The Heinemann Illustrated Encyclopedia

Volume 9
Slu-Tor

Heinemann
LIBRARY

First published in Great Britain by Heinemann Library
Halley Court, Jordan Hill, Oxford OX2 8EJ
a division of Reed Educational and Professional Publishing Ltd.

OXFORD MELBOURNE AUCKLAND
JOHANNESBURG BLANTYRE GABORONE
IBADAN PORTSMOUTH NH (USA) CHICAGO

Series Editors: Rebecca and Stephen Vickers
Author Team: Rob Alcraft, Catherine Chambers, Jim Drake,
Fred Martin, Angela Royston, Jane Shuter, Roger Thomas,
Rebecca Vickers, Stephen Vickers
Reading Consultant: Betty Root

Photo research by Katharine Smith
Designed and Typeset by Gecko Ltd
Printed in Hong Kong by Wing King Tong

02 01 00 99 98
10 9 8 7 6 5 4 3 2 1

ISBN 0 431 09060 2

British Library Cataloguing in Publication Data.

The Heinemann illustrated encyclopedia
1. Children's encyclopedias and dictionaries
I. Vickers, Rebecca II. Vickers, Stephen, 1951–
032

ISBN 0431090629

Acknowledgements:
Cover: The cover illustration is of a male specimen of *Ornithoptera goliath*, commonly called the
Goliath Birdwing. Special thanks to Dr George C. McGavin and the Hope Entomological
Collections, Oxford University Museum of Natural History.

J. Allan Cash Ltd: pp8b, 14, 16L, 17, 21, 25t, 29b, 30, 33, 34, 35, 36, 41. **Ancient Art and
Architecture:** p26b; Brian Wilson – p26t. **Trevor Clifford Photography:** pp25b, 37b. **BBC Natural
History Unit:** Jeff Foott – p48b. **Bruce Coleman Ltd.:** Gunter Ziesler – p7b. **The Hutchison
Library:** Andrew Hill – p42t; Ingrid Hudson – p12; Trevor Page – p10. **Oxford Scientific Films:**
Kathie Atkinson – p8t; Niall Benvie – p20t; Neil Bromhall – p4b; Pat Clay – p45b; J.A.L. Cooke –
pp6b, 18r, 40r; E.R. Degginer – p20b; Jack Dermid — p45t; Fredrik Ehrenstrom – p23t; Sally and
Richard Greenhill – p27b; Richard Kolar – p44b; Pat and Tom Leeson – p32b; Tom McHugh – p19t;
Mantis Wildlife – p18t; Andrew J. Martinez – p19b; NASA – p22b (Warren Faidley); Rob
Nunnington – p40L; Kjell Sandved – p23b; Frank Schneidermeyer – p43b; Donald Specker – p4t;
Survival Anglia – p13 (Dr F. Koster); Tony Tilford – p32t. **Redferns:** Mick Hutson — p28b. **Science
Photo Library:** ESA – p31b; David Hardy – pp9, 15t; Library of Congress – p38b; Richard Megna –
p11b; Hank Morgan – p11t; NASA – p15b, p16r; Francoise Sauze – p38t. **Shakespeare's Globe:**
John Tramper – p42b. **Tony Stone Images:** John Elk – p28t; David Sams – p47.

Every effort has been made to contact copyright holders of any material
reproduced in this book. Any omissions will be rectified in subsequent printings
if notice is given to the Publisher.

Welcome to the
Heinemann Illustrated Encyclopedia

What is an encyclopedia?

An encyclopedia is an information book. It gives the most important facts about a lot of different subjects. This encyclopedia has been specially written for children your age. It covers many of the subjects from school and others you may find interesting.

What is in this encyclopedia?

In this encyclopedia each topic is called an entry. There is one page for every entry. The entries in this encyclopedia are on:

- animals
- plants
- dinosaurs
- countries
- geography
- history
- world religions
- music
- art
- transport
- science
- technology

How to use this encyclopedia

This encyclopedia has eleven books, called volumes. The first ten volumes contain entries. The entries are all in alphabetical order. This means that Volume One starts with entries that begin with the letter 'A' and Volume Ten ends with entries that begin with the letter 'Z'. Volume Eleven is the index volume and has some other interesting information in its Fact Finder section.

Here are two entries, showing you what you can find on a page:

This is the letter that the entry starts with.

Fact boxes give you details about the topic.

The See also line tells you where to find other related information.

Did You Know? boxes have fun or interesting bits of information.

The Fact File tells you important facts and figures.

Slug

See also: Mollusc, Snail

A slug is a small, slow animal with a soft body. Slugs are in the group of animals called molluscs. They have no bones and no legs. Slugs slither along on one big foot. Some slugs live on land and others live in water.

Slug families

There are no male and female slugs. Instead, each slug is both male *and* female all in one. Every adult slug can lay eggs.

Slugs move slowly over the ground using their feelers to find their favourite food. Slugs like damp, cool places because they can easily dry out and die.

The slug's big foot leaves a slimy trail on the ground to help the rest of its body to slip along.

SLUG FACTS

NUMBER OF KINDS	over 35,000 kinds of slug and snail
COLOUR	black, brown or brightly coloured
SIZE	up to 10 cm long
STATUS	common
LIFE SPAN	up to 7 years
ENEMIES	mammals such as hedgehogs and shrews

Soft, slimy body

Feelers taste and smell the air

A grey garden slug

FOOD

Slugs come out to feed mostly at night. They eat shoots, lichen, fungi and algae. Slugs can't chew. A slug has a special rough tongue, like a nail file. This grates up the food into little pieces.

Slug eggs are laid near food so the babies have plenty to eat.

Smell

See also: Taste

Smell is one of the senses that help animals and people find out about things around them. Human beings and some other animals use their noses to smell things by sniffing the air.

How smelling works

Nearly everything has some smell. When air is taken into the nose, cells in the nose send signals to the brain. As animals or humans get used to using their noses, they get to know the smell of different objects.

DID YOU KNOW?

Dogs are used by the police to find missing or lost people. A specially trained dog is given something used by the missing person, then it follows the scent trail to the person.

Using smells

People smell food to make sure it is fit to eat. The sense of smell can also warn people of danger, such as smoke when there is a fire, or the smell of gas if there is a leak. Animals use their sense of smell to help them find the food they need, to find a mate and to know if enemies are near. Some animals use scents to mark their territory, or to find their way back to their homes.

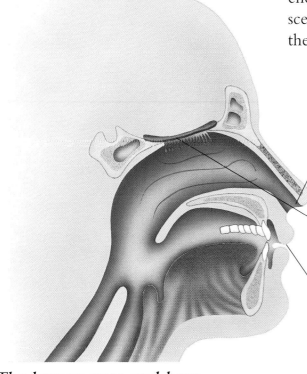

Air is taken in through the nostrils into the nasal passages

The air passes cells called smell receptors. These send messages about the smell to the brain

Air taken in through the mouth does not pass the smell receptors. So, the brain does not get sent any messages about the smell

The human nose and how smelling works.

Snail

See also: Mollusc, Slug

A snail is a small, slow animal with a soft body. Snails belong to the group of animals called molluscs. Snails have no legs, but slither along on one big foot. They carry their shells on their backs. Snails live all over the world, in water and on land.

Snail families

There are no male or female snails. Instead, each snail is a male *and* a female all in one. Every snail can lay eggs. It lays its eggs near plenty of food for the baby snails to eat when they hatch.

SNAIL FACTS

NUMBER OF	
KINDS..............	over 35,000 kinds of slug and snail
COLOUR	many colours
LENGTH..........	up to 60 cm
WEIGHT..........	up to 900 g
STATUS..........	common
LIFE SPAN........	up to 7 years
ENEMIES..........	birds, people

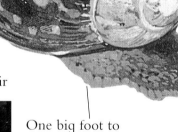

Shell to be the snail's home

A garden snail

Eyes on stalks

Feelers to taste and smell the air

One big foot to slither along on

These garden snail's eggs are just hatching.

FOOD

Snails eat plants and other snails. They can't chew. A snail has a special rough tongue, like a nail file. This grates up the food into little pieces.

Snake

See also: Reptile

A snake is an animal with no legs and a long, thin body. Snakes are reptiles. They live all over the world, except in the very coldest places. Some snakes that live in cold places hibernate in the winter. Many snakes live on land. Some can live in water.

SNAKE FACTS

NUMBER OF KINDS	2000
COLOUR	many
LENGTH	up to 10 m
WEIGHT	up to 22 kg
STATUS	cobras are rare
LIFE SPAN	up to 30 years
ENEMIES	other snakes, people

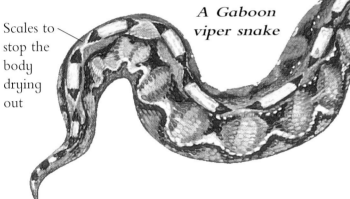

A Gaboon viper snake

Scales to stop the body drying out

Jaws that unhinge to open extra wide, to let the snake swallow big animals

Pointed head to help push through soft ground and thick plant growth

Snake families

Most female snakes lay up to ten eggs, and cover them over or bury them in the ground. The eggs hatch into baby snakes. Some snakes are born live, out of the mother, and do not hatch from eggs. The baby snakes look after themselves as soon as they are hatched or born.

FOOD

All snakes are hunters and eat meat. Snakes will eat mammals, birds and other reptiles. Snakes swallow their victims whole. After a meal, the food looks like a big lump being squeezed down through the snake's body.

Snakes have many ways of killing their food. The rattlesnake has a poisonous bite. The boa constrictor crushes its victims. This python has opened its jaw wide to swallow a whole gazelle.

Soil

See also: Crop, Farming

Soil is made up of broken bits of rock, minerals, plants and animals. It covers most solid ground in the world. It takes thousands of years for bigger pieces of rock, minerals and rotted plants and animals to form the small particles that make up the soil.

Different kinds of soil

Soil with lots of bits of dead plants and animals in it is called humus. Humus in soil helps to hold water. Many plants grow well in humus. When plants grow well in soil, farmers and gardeners say that the soil is fertile.

Soil with very, very small particles is called clay. This kind of soil is very sticky. Clay soil can be used to make bricks or pottery. Sandy soils are made from larger particles. They are easy to dig, but to keep them fertile they must have humus or special chemicals called fertilizers added to them.

Plant roots hold soil together. If all the plants are cut down, soil can be blown or washed away. This is called erosion. This picture shows big gulleys made by erosion.

Huge fields for crops are made when trees and hedges are cut down.

DID YOU KNOW?

Worms help make the soil better for plants. They do this by making spaces in the soil for the air to get in, and by pulling parts of dead plants and animals down into the soil.

Solar system

See also: Planet, Star, Sun

A solar system is all of the objects, including planets, moons and asteroids, that orbit a star. The Earth's solar system is made up of the Sun (our star), nine planets and their moons, millions of asteroids and some comets.

Nicolaus Copernicus (1473–1543)

Before the Danish astronomer Copernicus wrote about what he saw in the sky, people believed that everything in the sky moved around the Earth. Copernicus showed that the Earth and other planets moved around the Sun.

Solar systems and gravity

Solar systems are held together by gravity. All objects have gravity forces that pull other things towards them, but the gravity of larger objects is stronger than the force of smaller objects. The Sun's gravity pulls all the planets and keeps them in their orbits.

Our solar system probably started as a big cloud of gas and dust. Most of the gas formed the Sun. All of the gas and dust that was left over made the planets and comets.

In our solar system the planets near to the Sun – Mercury, Venus, Earth and Mars – are rocky and quite small. The planets further away – Jupiter, Saturn, Uranus and Neptune – are much bigger and not solid. Pluto is small even though it is the furthest from the Sun. The Sun's gravity probably pulled Pluto in after the other planets were in place. Between Mars and Jupiter there is a ring of smaller, rocky lumps, called asteroids.

All the planets in our solar system and the asteroid belt orbit the Sun. This model also shows a comet.

Somalia

See also: Africa

Somalia is a country in east Africa. It is flat and sandy along the coast. There are hills in the north. A small amount of rain falls between March and May. It is mostly very dry except in the south.

People from the surrounding small villages visit the markets in the bigger villages and towns.

Living and working

Most people in Somalia are nomads, so they do not stay in one place. Nomads need to move to find food and water for the herds of goats, sheep, cattle and camels that they keep. Their homes are made from skins or mats over wooden frames.

Many Somalis eat *anan geil.* This is millet cooked with camel milk and honey. Poetry, folk tales and history are very important. *Dab-Shid* is the Somali New Year festival of fire and light. It is celebrated with feasts and big bonfires.

DID YOU KNOW?

The ancient perfumes called frankincense and myrrh are collected as sap from trees in Somalia.

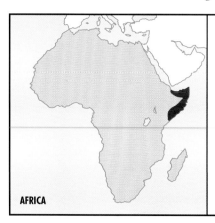

AFRICA

FACT FILE

PEOPLE	Somalis
POPULATION	9.1 million
MAIN LANGUAGES	Somali, Arabic
CAPITAL CITY	Mogadishu
MONEY	Somali shilling
HIGHEST MOUNTAIN	Mount Surad – 2408 m
LONGEST RIVER	Webi Shaballe – 1930 km

Sound

See also: Ear

Sounds are the noises that people and animals hear. They are caused by vibrations, which are tiny forward and backward movements. Sound waves made by the vibrations are picked up by the ears of humans and animals. Sound travels in invisible waves through air, through liquids and through solids.

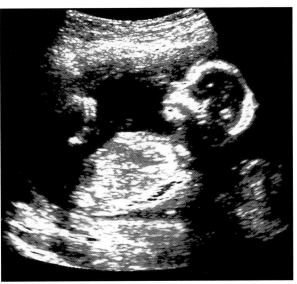

This ultrasound picture was made by echoes bouncing off a baby inside its mother.

Kinds of sound

Different kinds of vibrations make different sounds. Most sounds are a mixture of vibrations. In loud sounds the vibrations are big. Sounds like the noise made by a whistle have very quick vibrations. Sounds like thunder have slow vibrations.

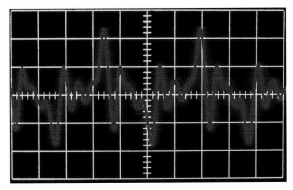

Everything, from a human voice to a musical instrument, has its own special pattern of vibrations. This red line shows the sound waves of a note being played by a harmonica.

Speed of sound

Sound travels over 300 metres in a second. This is a speed of about 1200 kph. It is now possible for cars and aeroplanes to travel faster than sound. They can overtake the sound they make. If sound hits something hard, such as a wall or a cliff, it will bounce off. When the sound travels back to where it was made, you hear an echo.

DID YOU KNOW?

Some sounds are so high-pitched that the human ear cannot hear them. This type of sound is called ultrasonic or ultrasound. Ultrasound is used by doctors to make echoes inside the human body. Special machines make pictures of what is inside the body, using the echoes of the ultrasound.

South Africa

See also: Africa

South Africa is a country in Africa. Most of it is high, flat land. The north-west has hot, dry deserts. In the south there are mountains. It rains from October to April.

Living and working

About half the people in South Africa live in cities. Mining is very important. In the countryside, farmers raise animals, and grow cereals and fruit.

The people in South Africa are a mix of local black Africans and the families of the Dutch, British and Asian people who have moved to South Africa over the last 300 years. The customs, food and religions of all of these peoples can be seen in the country today.

Townships like this one grew up around all of the big towns and cities in South Africa. This happened during the time when black South Africans weren't allowed to live in the cities.

DID YOU KNOW?

Nelson Mandela was elected as the country's first black president. He fought for the rights of black South Africans. Mandela spent 27 years in prison for his beliefs.

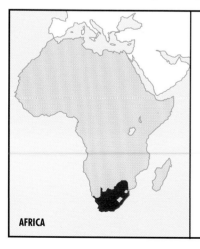

AFRICA

FACT FILE

PEOPLE....................... South Africans
POPULATION............... 40.6 million
MAIN LANGUAGES .... Afrikaans, English, African languages
CAPITAL CITY.............. Pretoria
LARGEST CITY.............. Cape Town
MONEY....................... Rand
HIGHEST MOUNTAIN... Thaban-Ntlenyana – 3482 m
LONGEST RIVER........... Orange River – 1860 km

South America

See also: Continent

South America is the fourth biggest continent. The Atlantic Ocean is along the east coast. The Pacific Ocean is along the west coast.

The land

The Andes Mountains stretch the whole length of South America along the western side. Some of the highest mountains are active volcanoes. The River Amazon and many smaller rivers flow across the flat land in the north.

Climate, plants and animals

It is always hot and wet in the Amazon area. Most of the land around the River Amazon is covered by rainforest. Animals such as monkeys, armadillos and some hummingbirds live in the rainforest. Grasslands in the south are called the pampas.

People in South America

There are about 310 million people in South America. Some are native Indian peoples. Others are the descendants of people from Spain and Portugal. There are also descendants of slaves from Africa. This mix of people now live together in thirteen different countries.

SOUTH AMERICA FACTS

SIZE	17.8 million square km
HIGHEST MOUNTAIN	Aconcagua – 6959 m
LONGEST RIVER	River Amazon – 6450 km
SPECIAL FEATURE	Angel Falls in Venezuela is the world's highest waterfall
BIGGEST COUNTRY	Brazil

The huge bird called the Andean Condor can be seen flying high over many countries in South America. It has a wingspan of over three metres.

South Korea

See also: Asia, North Korea

South Korea is a country on the east coast of Asia. Most of South Korea is covered by hills and mountains. There are thousands of small islands off the west coast. The weather is cold and dry in the winter. Summer months are hot and very wet.

DID YOU KNOW?

The 1988 summer Olympic Games were held in Seoul, the capital city of South Korea.

Living and working

Most people work in offices and in factories. South Korea makes ships, cars and electrical goods. These goods are sold all over the world. Farmers grow rice and vegetables. Mulberries are also grown, to feed to silkworms.

The people in South Korea are very proud of their past. There are many traditional Korean customs and special music and dances. The martial arts sport of *tae'kwondo* comes from South Korea.

In this small town near the capital city, Seoul, the people live in small houses with different coloured roofs.

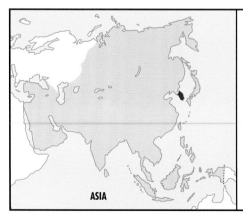

ASIA

FACT FILE

PEOPLE .... South Koreans
POPULATION .... 44.6 million
MAIN LANGUAGE .... Korean
CAPITAL CITY .... Seoul
MONEY .... South Korean won
HIGHEST MOUNTAIN ... Halla-san – 1950 m
LONGEST RIVER .... River Han – 470 km

Space exploration

See also: Planet, Spacecraft

People have looked out into space since ancient times. But people have only been able to go into space for a few decades. Even today, most space exploration is done using telescopes or robot probes.

The first space exploration

In 1957, the first satellite, *Sputnik 1,* was sent up by the Russians. Only twelve years later the American *Apollo 11* mission put men on the moon. Space probes have now been to all of the planets except for Pluto. Other probes have flown close to comets.

This is an artist's drawing of Sputnik 1, the first man-made satellite to orbit the Earth. It was made of aluminium and had four hanging aerials.

This robot was used in 1997 in the unmanned exploration of Mars.

Telescopes

Telescopes can be used to see objects millions of kilometres away in space. People have been able to explore space by looking through telescopes since the first telescope was invented in 1608. They have become much bigger and more powerful. All the comets that are known about have been discovered by people looking through telescopes.

DID YOU KNOW?

A person who studies space is called an astronomer.

Spacecraft

See also: Moon, Space exploration

A spacecraft is a machine that travels into space. Unmanned spacecraft have no people inside. Manned spacecraft carry people inside them. People that go into space are called astronauts.

The first spacecraft

The first spacecraft to carry a person into space was launched in 1961. Just like spacecraft today, it was fixed to a large rocket and fired into space. Most spacecraft do not carry people. They take computers and other scientific equipment. They send back to Earth pictures and information about the places they visit.

SPACECRAFT FIRSTS

FIRST SPACECRAFT.....	*Sputnik 1,* 1957
FIRST PERSON IN SPACE....................	Yuri Gagarin, Soviet Union (Russia), April 1961
FIRST AMERICAN ASTRONAUT...............	Alan Shepard Jr, USA, May 1961
FIRST MANNED MOONLANDING.........	US Apollo 11 mission, 1969
FIRST TRIP BY US SPACE SHUTTLE.........	12 April 1981

How we use spacecraft

Spacecraft can take pictures of far away planets. Spacecraft, such as satellites, can be used for sending TV pictures and telephone calls around the world.

The US space shuttle takes off attached to a large launch rocket.

American astronauts on the moon used a little electric vehicle, called the moon buggy, to travel around in.

Spain

See also: Europe

Spain is a country in southwest Europe. There is a high, flat area in the centre. It is crossed by mountain ranges. Summers are hot and dry. Winters can be cold, with some snow.

Living and working

Many people in Spain live in the cities. They work in offices, factories and in the tourist trade. Farmers grow crops such as wheat, oranges and olives. They also raise animals.

A popular Spanish meal is *paella*. This is rice cooked with a spice called saffron, and mixed with meat and fish. The saffron makes the rice turn yellow.

For at least 500 years a dance called the flamenco has been performed in Southern Spain. The dancers wear special, colourful outfits. It is a mix of gypsy and North African dance.

Building of this cathedral in Barcelona was started in 1883. It is not finished yet because the architect died without leaving any plans.

DID YOU KNOW?

The famous modern artist Pablo Picasso (1881–1973) was born in Spain. Many people think that Picasso is the most important artist of the 20th century.

EUROPE

FACT FILE

PEOPLE	Spanish, Spaniards
POPULATION	39.6 million
MAIN LANGUAGES	Spanish, Catalan, Galician, Basque
CAPITAL CITY	Madrid
MONEY	Peseta
HIGHEST MOUNTAIN	Mulhacén – 3478 m
LONGEST RIVER	Guadiana – 829 km

Spider

See also: Invertebrate

A spider is a small animal with eight legs. Many spiders spin strong but delicate-looking webs to catch food. Spiders have been on the Earth since the time of the dinosaurs.

Spider families

Female spiders lay eggs that hatch into baby spiders. Spider babies are called spiderlings. Until they grow to full size, they cannot hunt or spin webs.

When a spider traps an animal in its web, it bites it. Spiders have pointed fangs, like teeth. The fangs are sharp, and pump the victim full of poison.

SPIDER FACTS

NUMBER OF KINDS	over 30,000
COLOUR	mostly brown or black
LENGTH	up to 28 cm from leg tip to leg tip
STATUS	common
LIFE SPAN	18 months – 25 years
ENEMIES	birds, wasps, other spiders

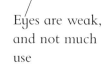

Tubes to make silk for spinning webs

Hairs on the body and legs to help the spider see and hear

Some spiderlings travel on their mother's back

Eyes are weak, and not much use

A wolf spider

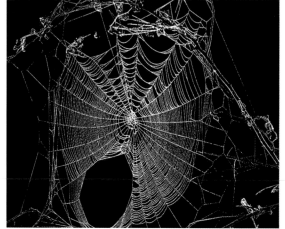

Spiders use their webs to trap and store food.

FOOD

Spiders mainly eat insects, although some very big spiders can eat small birds. Without spiders the world would have far too many insects. Some spiders have bites that are so poisonous they can kill people.

Squid

See also: Mollusc

A squid is a type of mollusc. It is an invertebrate. Squid live mostly in warm seas. Some are tiny, but the giant squid can be 18 m long. The squid squirts a black liquid called ink at its enemies, so they cannot see and the squid can escape.

SQUID FACTS

NUMBER OF KINDS	over 300
COLOUR	can change colour.
LENGTH	up to 18 m
STATUS	common
LIFE SPAN	2–5 years
ENEMIES	fish, seals and whales; people

Squid families

Most squid get together in large groups to mate. These groups are called shoals. The female squid lays about 2000 eggs and sticks them to seaweed or rocks. After three or four weeks the baby squid hatch. They take care of themselves. After two years, they are fully grown.

Under the skin is a shell for extra protection

Large eyes to see well under the sea

Ten tentacles with suckers for catching food

A Californian market squid

These long-finned squid are on the bottom of the sea with a newly laid mass of eggs.

FOOD

A squid eats mostly fish and creatures with shells. It catches a fish by holding it with its long tentacles and paralyzing it with a special poison.

Squirrel

See also: Mammal

A squirrel is a small mammal with a bushy tail. Squirrels have large eyes, and strong legs and claws. They use their big front teeth for nibbling bark and nuts. Squirrels live in most parts of the world.

SQUIRREL FACTS

NUMBER OF KINDS	over 70
COLOUR	red, brown, grey, beige
LENGTH	13–90 m
WEIGHT	9 g–8 kg
STATUS	common
LIFE SPAN	2–10 years
ENEMIES	birds of prey, foxes, people

Bushy tail for balance while running and jumping

A red squirrel

Big front teeth for nibbling through bark and shells

Paws for gripping food

Squirrel families

A female squirrel has several babies at a time. Both parents look after the babies in a nest that they build, called a drey.

There are many different kinds of squirrel. Red and grey squirrels live in trees. The flying squirrel has big flaps of skin that it can hold out, like an open coat. It glides from tree to tree. Ground squirrels and prairie dogs live in holes or burrows under ground.

FOOD

Squirrels eat bark, nuts, mushrooms, seeds and some insects. They hide food for the winter.

These baby grey squirrels will be looked after by their parents until they are older.

Sri Lanka

See also: Asia

Sri Lanka is a country in south Asia. It is made up of one big island, with some smaller islands. The north is flat. There are mountains at the centre of the big island. The areas of lower ground are hot and wet.

Living and working

Most people in Sri Lanka live in the countryside, growing rice, coconuts, rubber and tea. They often eat rice, cooked with mango, coconut and peanuts. Coconuts, cloves and cinnamon are used to flavour bean, meat and fish dishes. In the cities chemicals and building materials are made.

Sri Lankan dancing is very famous. Each small movement has a meaning. There is a lot of dancing at the *Perahara* festival, a torchlight procession with decorated elephants.

The dance being performed in this photo is called Kandyan dance. It is named after the city of Kandy. Kandyan dance is the national dance-drama of Sri Lanka.

DID YOU KNOW?

Until 1972 Sri Lanka was called Ceylon.

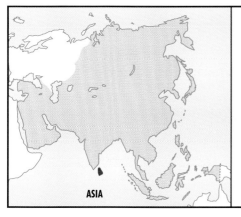

ASIA

FACT FILE

PEOPLE	Sri Lankans
POPULATION	18.1 million
MAIN LANGUAGES	Sinhala, Tamil, English
CAPITAL CITY	Colombo
MONEY	Sri Lankan rupee
HIGHEST MOUNTAIN	Pidurutalagala – 2524 m
LONGEST RIVER	Mahaweli Ganga – 210 km

Star

See also: Solar system, Sun

Stars are huge balls of burning gas. The Sun is the star at the centre of our solar system. Stars look small because they are so far away. Some stars are much bigger than our Sun.

The night sky

Thousands of stars can be seen in the sky. Some look brighter than others. Some stars also seem to be different colours. Bluish stars are the hottest. Yellow stars are the coolest.

Stars are so far away that light from them takes years to reach Earth. Distances between stars are often measured in the number of years it takes the light to reach Earth. One light-year is the distance travelled by light in one year. The nearest stars are about four light-years away, about 40,000,000,000,000 km!

The Andromeda galaxy contains millions of stars.

DID YOU KNOW?

People have always seen patterns in the stars in the night skies. These patterns are called constellations. Many are named after heroes and gods from ancient times.

1 First it is a large cloud of gases

2 It becomes smaller and hotter and starts to shine

3 As it burns itself up over thousands of millions of years it swells into a 'red giant'

4 The star may explode and end up as a 'white dwarf'

Stages in the life of a star.

Starfish

See also: Invertebrate, Sea life

A starfish is a sea animal. It has five bendy legs and is star-shaped. Its skin is bony and hard. Starfish live in seas all over the world.

Starfish families

Starfish babies come from millions of tiny eggs which the starfish sends floating out into the sea. These settle in rock pools and hatch into tiny rectangular larvae. The larvae float about in the sea until they grow into adult starfish.

STARFISH FACTS

NUMBER OF KINDS	1600
COLOUR	all colours
LENGTH	1 cm – 1 m across
STATUS	common
LIFE SPAN	about 6 years
ENEMIES	fish, other starfish

Suckers on each foot for gripping rocks and food

Strong, bendy legs to hold food

Eyes at the end of each leg that see only light and dark

Mouth on the underside at the centre

A common starfish

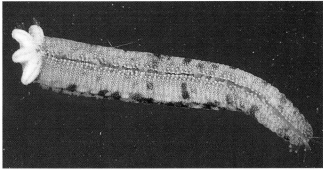

A starfish can grow back lost parts of its body. This single leg is growing another complete body.

FOOD

Starfish are hunters. They eat mussels and other sea animals with shells. A starfish puts its arms round its food and slowly pulls the shell open. It then pushes its stomach into the shell and begins to eat.

Stegosaur

See also: Dinosaur, Fossil

A stegosaur was a four-legged dinosaur with big, boney plates sticking up along its back. On its tail it had long spikes. The stegosaur was about three metres high and about as heavy as a modern-day rhinoceros.

STEGOSAUR FACTS

LENGTH.... **about** 9 m
WEIGHT.... 2 tonnes
ENEMIES.... big meat-eating dinosaurs such as the allosaur

FOOD

The stegosaur only ate plants. It had a small mouth, a bit like a beak. It could eat plants off the ground, or it may have stood up on its back legs to reach branches.

Lifestyle

The stegosaur's big, bony plates probably helped it stay at the right temperature. If the plates faced the Sun, they would help the stegosaur soak up the Sun's rays and warm up. If the plates faced away from the Sun they would help it cool down.

A Stegosaur

Bony plates for defence and keeping cool

Teeth with ridges to help chew plants

Spikes on the tail to fend off attacks from enemies

Stem

See also: Plant

A stem is the part of the plant from which the leaves and flowers grow. The stem carries water from the roots to the leaves. It takes food made in the leaves to the rest of the plant.

How a stem grows

Most stems grow above the ground. The main stem pushes up from the seed through the soil. Sometimes the main stem splits into thinner branch stems. Some plants have underground stems that form thick, swollen ends called bulbs or tubers. Tulips, daffodils and crocuses all grow from bulbs. The potatoes people eat are tubers.

Bamboo is the fastest-growing plant. Its stems can grow almost a metre in a day. The stems of bamboo are used to build houses and furniture in some countries.

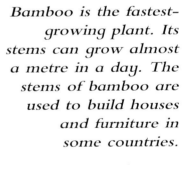

People eat the main stems of asparagus and celery. Potatoes and onions are swollen underground stems.

Stone Age

See also: Bronze Age, Iron Age

The Stone Age is the time in a country's history when people made tools and weapons from stone, especially flint. It started and finished at different times in different countries. The Stone Age is the earliest time in the history of people. The Stone Age in Europe lasted over two million years.

Why was the Stone Age important?

The Stone Age was important because it was the time when the first people on Earth found out how to live and work together. During the Stone Age people learned how to speak. They found out how to use fire to keep warm and to cook food. They started to sew animal skins together to make clothes. They began to paint pictures on walls, even though they could not write.

KEY DATES

2,000,000 BC... People began to use stone tools

1,500,000 BC... The first stone axes were made

75,000 BC........ People started to use fire

20,000 BC........ People began to use bows and arrows. They made bone needles and sewed skins to make clothes. They made paintings in caves

6000 BC........... People in the Middle East began to use copper. There, the Stone Age had ended

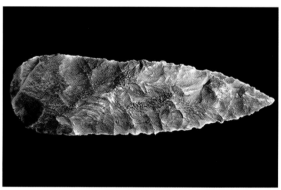

This flint spearhead was made about 6,500 years ago. Tiny pieces of flint were chipped off to get the right shape.

What came next?

Stone tools and weapons took a long time to make. They could break easily. It was not always easy to find the right sort of stone. The best tools are made with a hard stone, called flint. Stone Age people learned how to use metal for tools and weapons instead. The first metal they used was copper.

This stone axe head is made of polished flint.

Story

See also: Literature

A story is a way of telling people about a series of events. If the story is made up, it is called fiction. A story about true events is called non-fiction. Stories can be written down or spoken from memory. People who write stories are called authors. Some stories are put into books. Some of these may have pictures, drawn by illustrators.

What is a story?

Whether it is true or made up, a story usually has a plot. This is the beginning, middle and end of the story. It also has characters. These are the people or animals that take part in the events in the story. All stories have settings. The setting is the time and place where the story happens.

This is a picture from a story called **Gulliver's Travels,** *about a man who visits lots of strange places.*

Kinds of stories

Fiction stories have many different settings. Sometimes stories are divided into types by their setting. Fantasies are stories set in times and places that are made up, and they may include magic. Historical fiction is set in a time in the past. Science fiction is often set in a time in the future. Mysteries and detective stories have a crime or mystery for the characters to solve.

Reading aloud from a book is a popular way of passing on a story.

Stringed instruments

See also: Music, Musical instrument, Orchestra

Stringed instruments are musical instruments that make sounds when strings are plucked, strummed, rubbed or struck.

The first stringed instruments

The earliest stringed instrument was probably a hunter's bow, which made a twanging sound when the string was plucked. Instruments like this are still used today in Africa. The player taps the string with a stick held in one hand. The notes change by bending the bow and stretching the string.

Types of stringed instruments

Stringed instruments are divided up depending on how they are played. Bowed string instruments have strings that are rubbed to make the sound, using a bow fitted with sticky hair. The violin, cellos and the Indian *sarangi* are bowed instruments.

Plucked string instruments are twanged, using the fingers and thumb. They include the guitar, the harp and the African *kora*. Strummed string instruments have the strings brushed with the fingers, or with something held in the fingers. The guitar, the dulcimer and the ukelele are strummed.

This Korean man is playing a traditional string instrument called a koto.

This is violinist, Vanessa-Mae. The violin was invented in Europe but is used in the music of many countries.

DID YOU KNOW?

One type of bass guitar has strings made from a kind of artificial rubber.

Submarine

See also: Ship, Transport

A submarine is a boat that can travel under water. When special tanks inside it are filled with air, a submarine can float. If the air is let out the submarine will sink. The first submarines were built 350 years ago.

The first submarines

The first submarine was made of wood and powered by oars. It was rowed under water along the River Thames, near London. Today submarines are built of steel. They are large and powerful and can stay under water for months.

SUBMARINE FACTS

FIRST SUBMARINE	built in 1620
FIRST HAND-POWERED	1876
FIRST STEAM-POWERED	1880
FIRST GAS/ELECTRIC-POWERED	1890s
FIRST NUCLEAR-POWERED	1955
BIGGEST	Russian *Typhoon* class submarine
GREATEST DEPTH	11,000 m

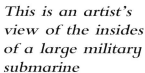

This is an artist's view of the insides of a large military submarine

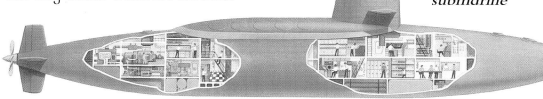

How we use submarines

Most submarines are used by navies. They can attack ships and even cities. Smaller submarines called submersibles are used to explore the deep sea, and repair oil rigs.

DID YOU KNOW?

In 1958 the US nuclear-powered submarine *Nautilus* went under the North Pole.

Submersibles, like this one, carry out scientific work. They can usually only take two to three passengers.

Sudan

See also: Africa

Sudan is a country in northeast Africa. There is desert in the north. In the centre there is farm land with hills. The west has mountains. In the south, there are hot, wet swamps and rainforest. It rains in summer.

Living and working

Over half the people in Sudan are farmers who live in the countryside, raising animals and growing crops. A common food in Sudan is sorghum and spiced vegetables. Sorghum is an important crop in all the dry areas of Africa. It is a grain that can be grown without much water. Some Sudanese are nomads. They move from place to place looking for food for their animals.

These nomads are travelling with all their household goods loaded on a camel.

DID YOU KNOW?

Sudan is the largest country in Africa. It is about 1030 km from north to south. It is about 625 km from east to west.

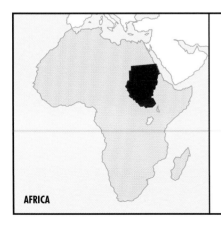

AFRICA

FACT FILE

PEOPLE	Sudanese
POPULATION	27.4 million
MAIN LANGUAGES	Arabic, African languages
CAPITAL CITY	Khartoum
MONEY	Dinar
HIGHEST MOUNTAIN	Mount Kinyeti – 3187 m
LONGEST RIVER	River Nile – 6670 km

Sun

See also: Solar system, Star

The Sun is the star in the centre of the Earth's solar system. It is a huge ball of burning gas that gives out the heat and light that makes life on Earth possible. All the planets of the solar system orbit or revolve around the Sun, held in position by the Sun's gravity.

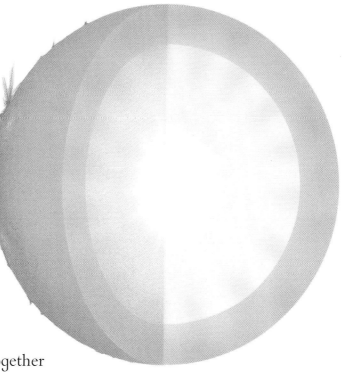

What is the Sun made of?

The Sun is a cloud of gas held together by gravity. It has been burning for over four billion years. It should burn for about another four billion years.

The Sun is very hot. At the centre, the temperature is about 20,000,000°C. The surface temperature is about 5600°C. There are slightly cooler patches called sunspots. These look less bright than the rest.

STAY SAFE!

Never stare at the Sun or look at the Sun through binoculars or a telescope. You could damage your eyes.

Sometimes huge flames up to 100,000 km long shoot out of the Sun. These are called solar prominences.

Swan

See also: Bird

The swan is the largest waterbird in the world. Swans live by lakes, rivers and canals. Some live at the seaside. Swans like living in areas where it doesn't get too hot or too cold. Some kinds of swan migrate.

Swan families

A male swan is called a cob. A female swan is called a pen. A baby swan is called a cygnet. A pen and a cob stay together for life. They build a nest on an island, in the reeds or on a beaver lodge to make it easier to keep enemies away.

The pen lays five or six eggs. The pen sits on the eggs and the cob brings her food. The cygnets stay with their parents for more than a year.

SWAN FACTS

NUMBER OF KINDS	7
COLOUR	white, black or black and white
LENGTH	up to 1.8 m
WEIGHT	up to 11.9 kg
STATUS	common
LIFE SPAN	up to 25 years
ENEMIES	Cygnets may be eaten by foxes and some fish

Wide beak for straining small weeds from the water

Long neck to reach plants under the water

Strong wings to fly a long way

A whooper swan

A mother keeps her cygnets close when out on the river.

FOOD

A swan eats water plants. With its long neck, it can reach plants that grow under the water. It will also eat grain crops in fields.

Sweden

See also: Europe

Sweden is a country in north-west Europe. There are cold, snow-covered mountains in the north. A high, flat area slopes down to the hilly coast. Summers are warm. Winters are cold and snowy.

The Swedish royal palace is in Old Stockholm.

Living and working

Most people in Sweden live in cities and large towns, where they work in offices and factories. Farmers grow grains and root crops, and raise cows for milk. Fish are caught around the Swedish coast. Herring is a popular fish to eat. There are many forests in the north. The trees are cut down for wood, and are used to make paper.

In Sweden, in April, the Feast of Valborg is held. Bonfires are an important part of this festival.

DID YOU KNOW?

At Christmas, Swedish girls dress up in white dresses, wearing wreaths of candles in their hair. They take their parents a special breakfast.

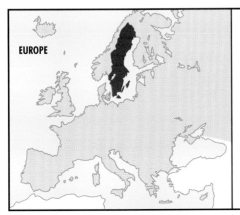

EUROPE

FACT FILE

PEOPLE...................... Swedes, Swedish
POPULATION.............. 8.7 million
MAIN LANGUAGE........ Swedish
CAPITAL CITY............. Stockholm
MONEY...................... Swedish krona
HIGHEST MOUNTAIN... Mount Kebnekaise – 2117 m
LONGEST RIVER......... Torne älve – 568 km

Switzerland

See also: Europe

Switzerland is a country in Europe. There are cold, snowy mountains in the south and north-west. Between the mountains there are valleys with many rivers and lakes, where it is warmer and not so wet.

Living and working

Most people in Switzerland live in towns and cities. Switzerland is famous for its watch and clock makers. Banking is also a very important business. Tourists visit Switzerland in the winter to ski. In the summer they climb and walk.

Farmers in Switzerland raise a lot of dairy cattle. The milk is used to make cheeses and chocolates. The Swiss eat many cheeses with different types of bread. They also enjoy eating fried, grated potato.

The overhanging roof of this house keeps the snow away from the windows and doors. This style of house is sometimes called a chalet.

DID YOU KNOW?

On Swiss stamps, you can see the word 'Helvetia'. This is the name of Celtic people who lived in the region long ago.

EUROPE

FACT FILE

PEOPLE........................Swiss

POPULATION...............7.1 million

MAIN LANGUAGES........German, French, Italian, Romansch

CAPITAL CITY.............Bern

BIGGEST CITY.............Zurich

MONEY.......................Swiss franc

HIGHEST MOUNTAIN... Matterhorn – 4478 m

LONGEST RIVER..........River Rhine – 1320 km

Syria

See also: Asia

Syria is a country in the Middle East. There are hills and mountains to the west. High, flat land slopes down to a river plain in the east. There are hot, dry desert areas. It is cooler in the hills. The coast is warm and wet.

Living and working

About half the people in Syria live in towns and cities. There is mining for oil and phosphates. Factories make food and cloth. Farmers in Syria grow cotton, grains, olives, beans and fruit. They also raise sheep, goats, cattle and donkeys.

Syria is a very ancient country. Its capital city, Damascus, is the oldest city with people still living in it. Today almost all of the people in Syria arc followers of Islam.

This is the entrance to one of the covered markets known as a bazaar or a souk.

DID YOU KNOW?

Damask is a kind of patterned fabric that is all one colour. It was named after the silks made in Damascus and taken to Europe by traders, hundreds of years ago.

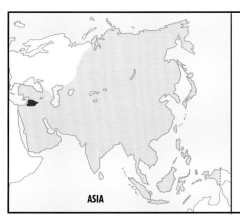

ASIA

FACT FILE

PEOPLE...................... Syrians

POPULATION............... 14.2 million

MAIN LANGUAGE......... Arabic

CAPITAL CITY............. Damascus

MONEY...................... Syrian pound

HIGHEST MOUNTAIN... Jabal ash-Shaykh – 2814 m

LONGEST RIVER.......... River Euphrates – 2700 km

Taiwan

See also: Asia, China

Taiwan is an island country in the east of Asia. The east has mountains with forests. The west is farm land. Summers are hot and humid. Winters are mild and wet, with hurricanes.

Living and working

Most people in Taiwan live in towns and cities. They work in offices and factories. In the countryside, farmers grow rice, fruit, tea and soya beans. Fish are caught in the sea around Taiwan. The people of Taiwan eat dried fish, fried with peanuts. They also make oyster omelettes.

Almost all of the people in Taiwan are Chinese. Ancient Chinese festivals are celebrated. Boats with dragons' heads are raced in the Dragon Boat Festival held every year.

This old Royal Palace in Taipei is now a museum.

DID YOU KNOW?

The island of Taiwan is also known as Formosa. Portuguese traders gave it this name in 1590. It means 'beautiful one'.

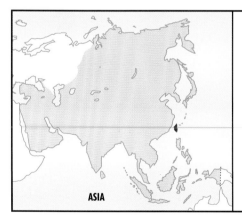

ASIA

FACT FILE

PEOPLE........................ Taiwanese
POPULATION .... 20.7 million
MAIN LANGUAGE......... Mandarin Chinese
CAPITAL CITY.............. Taipei
MONEY....................... New Taiwan dollar
HIGHEST MOUNTAIN... Mount Yu Shan – 3997 m
LONGEST RIVER........... Choshui – 200 km

Taste

See also: Smell

Taste is one of the five senses.
Tiny bumps on the tongue,
called taste buds, can tell the
brain if something inside the
mouth is salty, bitter, sweet
or sour.

The four tastes

There are four different types of taste
bud on the human tongue. When the
right sort of food lands on that taste bud
it sends a message to the brain. Some
taste buds can sense sweet things. Others
can sense salt or sour tastes. The very
back of the tongue senses bitter tastes.

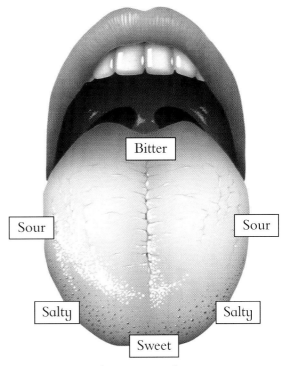

*Different places on the tongue can
sense the four types of taste.*

*Different foods have
different tastes.*

Taste and smell

The sense of taste is helped by the sense
of smell. Some foods are really given
their 'taste' by how they smell. When
food is chewed the smell gets into the
nose. If the nose is pinched closed, most
things taste the same.

DID YOU KNOW?

Things that taste bitter are sometimes bad
to eat. The bitter taste is a warning.

Telephone

See also: Communication

A telephone is a machine that lets you speak to someone when you are not with them. People can use a telephone to speak to friends next door or on the other side of the world.

The first telephone

The telephone was invented by the Scottish scientist Alexander Graham Bell, in the United States in 1876. He worked out that an electric current could be used to send the human voice from one place to another.

This modern telephone has a casing made of clear plastic, so you can see the insides.

Alexander Graham Bell, the inventor of the telephone, demonstrates his instrument in 1892.

Telephones today

Until the 1970s, all telephone calls went along wires. Cables carry telephone calls under the oceans. It is very expensive to lay the underwater cables. Satellite communication has made long-distance telephone calls cheaper. The signals travel up to the satellite and down again by radio waves. New communication methods, such as faxes, e-mail and the internet, all use the telephone system to send words and pictures instead of sounds.

DID YOU KNOW?

Mobile telephones use radio signals. Each mobile telephone has its own little receiver and transmitter for radio waves.

Television

See also: Communication, Radio

A television is a machine that can pick up radio waves and turn them into sounds and pictures. It is used for entertainment and to give out information, such as news and weather reports.

The first television

Two systems of television were invented by two different people: John Logie Baird and Vladimir Zworykin. At first, all TV shows were 'live', because there was no way of recording them. The pictures were fuzzy and small and in black and white. The first TV sets cost as much as a car.

Today, there are much bigger televisions and the pictures are in colour. New, wide-screen, digital and high-definition TV systems should give bigger and better pictures in future.

DID YOU KNOW?

The first television service started in Britain in 1936. It was in black and white. Colour television started in 1956 in the United States.

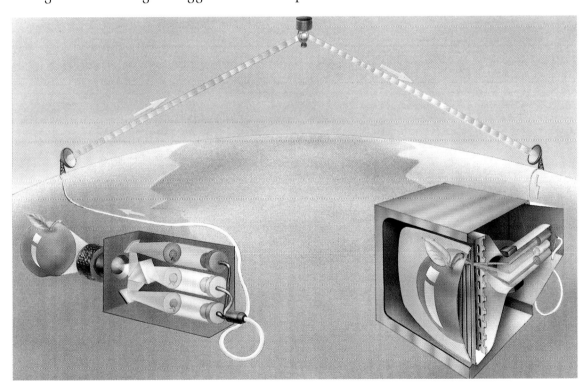

In satellite television, radio waves are sent out to a satellite orbiting the Earth. The signal then bounces back to Earth, sometimes thousands of miles from where the transmission started.

Termite

See also: Insect

A termite is a small, blind insect. Groups of termites build very large nests. Termites live all around the world, mainly in warm countries.

Termite families

Termites live in big groups called colonies. Two termites with wings fly off from one colony to start a new colony. They build a new, small nest. These two termites are called the king and the queen. The queen lays up to 30,000 eggs per day and gets very big. Most of these eggs hatch out as worker termites. They help to bring up the babies and make the nest bigger and bigger. Some of the eggs hatch as soldier termites. They protect the nest.

This huge mound was built by millions of tiny termites.

TERMITE FACTS

NUMBER OF KINDS	2300
COLOUR	brown or white
LENGTH	queen – up to 14 cm
	soldier – up to 2.2 cm
STATUS	common
LIFE SPAN	kings and queens – up to 10 years
ENEMIES	anteaters, pangolins, aardvarks, people

Antennae for smelling enemies

Powerful jaws for biting attackers

A termite soldier

FOOD

A termite eats wood. Its stomach is very good at digesting wood.

Thailand

See also: Asia

Thailand is a country in south-east Asia. There are mountains in the north and high, flat land in the east. Wide rivers flow through the centre. The weather is mostly hot with a dry season and a very wet season. There is forest over about one-third of Thailand.

Living and working

Most people in Thailand work on small farms where they grow rice, vegetables, cassava, maize and cotton. Some of the rice grown is sold to other countries. There is not much industry. Tourists visit Thailand to enjoy the beautiful beaches, Thai food, dancing and music. Most Thai food is cooked with spices, chillies and peppers. This makes it very hot and spicy.

Most people in Thailand are Buddhists. There are thousands of Buddhist shrines and temples.

Thai dancers still wear costumes like those worn hundreds of years ago.

DID YOU KNOW?

Some farmers use buffalo to pull ploughs in the rice fields.

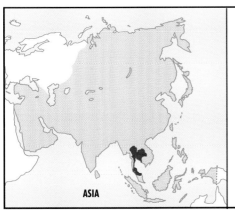

ASIA

FACT FILE

PEOPLE........................ Thais
POPULATION............... 58.2 million
MAIN LANGUAGE......... Thai
CAPITAL CITY..............Bangkok
MONEY....................... Baht
HIGHEST MOUNTAIN... Doi Inthanon – 2576 m
LONGEST RIVER...........Mekong River – 4500 km

Theatre

See also: Drama, Opera

The word 'theatre' is used for a building or place where plays, operas and ballets are performed. In ancient times, theatres were outdoors, open to the weather. The people who went to watch sat on raised seats in a big semi-circle.

Types of theatre

In some indoor theatres the people watching sit facing the performance, like in a cinema. In others, they can sit or stand all around the stage. This is sometimes called 'theatre in the round'. Any large area, such as a school hall or gymnasium, can be used as a theatre. The first known theatres in Europe were in Greece in 600 BC.

DID YOU KNOW?

The people who go to the theatre to watch a performance are called the audience.

This Ancient Greek theatre was outside. This type of theatre is called an ampitheatre.

This is the Globe Theatre, in London. It is a copy of the old Globe theatre built 400 years ago.

Tiger

See also: Mammal

Tigers are mammals. They are the largest and strongest members of the cat family. Tigers live in forests in Asia.

Tiger families

A male tiger is called a tiger. A female tiger is called a tigress. A tigress will have up to three cubs at a time. When the cubs are two to three years old, they will leave their mother. Each finds a part of the forest where they will live and hunt on their own.

Long tail for balance

Striped fur for moving through the trees without being seen

TIGER FACTS

NUMBER OF KINDS	8
COLOUR	golden-orange with black stripes
LENGTH	up to 3 m
WEIGHT	up to 270 kg
STATUS	endangered
LIFE SPAN	15 to 20 years
ENEMIES	people

A tiger

Razor-sharp teeth for killing and eating food

Sharp claws for climbing and for tearing food apart

Strong legs and body for running and pulling down victims

Like other members of the cat family, tigers groom themselves and their young.

FOOD

When tigers hunt they are patient and silent. They will follow their victims for great distances. They will hunt and eat most mammals in their territory.

Time

See also: Calendar, Measurement, Season

Time is the way people measure the periods between events. Some ways of counting time are natural, like day and night, or the seasons. Other ways of recording time have been invented by people to fit in with the cycles of nature.

Measuring time

There are different units of time. If something happens slowly, like when a person grows from a child to an adult, it can be measured in years. If it is quick, like a blink or a sneeze, it can be measured in seconds.

Clocks are used to measure time from day to day. The first clocks were sundials that cast shadows onto their face as the Sun moved across the sky. If the Sun wasn't shining, then the sundial didn't work. From the 1200s to the 1900s clocks became more and more accurate. Today, most clocks are electronic. The best clocks are atomic clocks that are so good that they only lose one second of time every thousand years.

DID YOU KNOW?

The Earth is divided up into 24 time zones. When it is 12 noon at midday in one place, on the other side of the world it is 12 midnight.

The atomic clock, in the middle of the photo, is the most accurate type of clock there is. The scientist in charge is wearing lots of other watches. None of them are as accurate.

The shadow on this sundial tells us it is half past ten.

Toad

See also: Amphibian, Frog

A toad is an amphibian. When it is an adult it lives on land, but it is born in the water. Toads have rough, spotty skin and short tongues. Some toads have poisonous skin. Different kinds of toad live in all but the very coldest areas of the world.

Toad families

Except in the breeding season, most toads live on their own. They spend the daytime hiding under stones or in burrows. Female toads lay strings of eggs, called toadspawn, in lakes or ponds. The eggs hatch into tadpoles. When the tadpoles lose their tails and grow legs, they are called toadlets.

TOAD FACTS

NUMBER OF KINDS	235
COLOUR	green or brown
LENGTH	up to 23 cm
WEIGHT	up to 1.5 kg
STATUS	common
LIFE SPAN	about 5 years
ENEMIES	birds, snakes, fish

Rough, tough skin to protect against bumps

Eyes on the top of the head, to look out of the water

Strong legs for jumping

An American toad

FOOD

A toad tadpole eats water plants and water insects. An adult toad hunts at night for insects and worms. Some kinds of big toads will even eat small snakes and birds.

Toadspawn is laid in strings, not clumps like frog spawn.

Tooth

See also: Human body

Teeth are used by humans and other animals to bite and chew food. If the teeth of humans, and most animals, get damaged, they can't grow new ones.

Kinds of teeth

Animals' teeth are specially adapted for the food they eat. Most animals have three types of teeth. At the front are incisors. These can snip and cut up food. To the side of the incisors are the canines. The canines are long, sharp teeth. Carnivores eat raw meat, and they have big canines to hold their prey and tear the meat off. Molars are the flatter teeth at the back of the mouth. They are used for grinding. Herbivores eat plants, and they have wide, flat molars to grind them up.

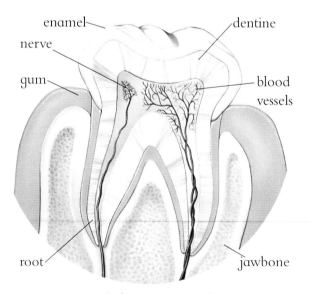

A human tooth

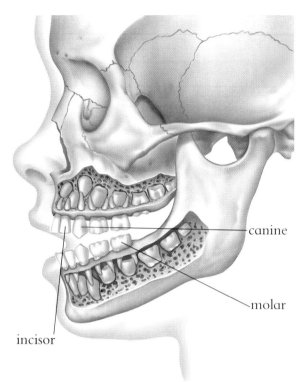

This shows the mouth of a child who still has baby teeth. You can see the adult teeth underneath waiting to push through.

Human teeth

When human beings are babies, a set of small teeth comes through. These are called milk teeth or baby teeth. These start to fall out as the permanent or adult teeth come through. These adult teeth have to last for the rest of the person's life.

DID YOU KNOW?

Bacteria in the mouth make acids that eat away at tooth enamel. This is called tooth decay. Cleaning the teeth and gums gets rid of bits of food and bacteria. A dentist can fill the holes in decaying teeth, but fillings don't last as well as enamel.

Tornado

See also: Hurricane, Weather

A tornado is a very powerful type of storm. The air twists around at very high speed. The air can be moving at speeds between 500 and 800 kph. A tornado is also sometimes called a twister.

The funnel cloud of this tornado, in the USA, is reaching down towards the ground.

How a tornado starts

A tornado is shaped like a narrow, twisting funnel. It is made from clouds and dust. The tornado stretches from the sky down to the ground. It can move across the land and may last for a few hours or only a few minutes.

Tornadoes begin to form over land when air starts to rise quickly. Some tornadoes begin over the sea. They are called waterspouts.

DID YOU KNOW?

There are so many tornadoes in the flat, central plains of North America that the area is called 'tornado alley'.

People and tornadoes

A tornado can wreck buildings, cars and roads. The damage can be terrible. Weather forecasters try to warn people, but is hard to know where tornadoes will go and how fast they will move. The safest place to be when a tornado strikes is in an underground shelter.

A tornado has completely destroyed this house.

Tortoise

See also: Reptile, Turtle

A tortoise is a reptile that has a hard shell. It can pull itself inside its shell for shelter or protection. There are several kinds of tortoise in the world. Most live in hot countries. On some islands, there are giant tortoises.

TORTOISE FACTS

NUMBER OF KINDS	40
COLOUR	brown
LENGTH	up to 1.4 m
WEIGHT	up to 245 kg
STATUS	some are threatened
LIFE SPAN	up to 200 years
ENEMIES	rats, cats, dogs, crabs and birds eat baby tortoises

Tortoise families

Adult tortoises do not look after baby tortoises. The female lays 10 to 20 round eggs and buries them in the sand or soil. The heat of the Sun keeps them warm. When the babies hatch they have to take care of themselves.

It can take many years for the babies to grow into full-size tortoises.

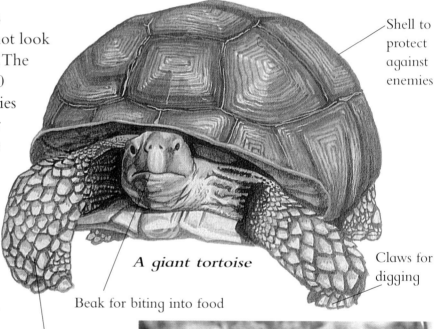

Shell to protect against enemies

A giant tortoise

Claws for digging

Beak for biting into food

Strong, scaly legs for walking

FOOD

A tortoise will eat almost any kind of food, although plant leaves and shoots are its favourite. A tortoise will even eat dead animals.

The desert tortoise eats when there has been rain and the plants grow quickly.